D0811549

Marion Public Library
1095 6th Avenue
Marion, IA 52302-3428
(319) 377-3412

EXTREME WEATHER

Hurricanes

by Kay Manolis

Consultant:
Mark Seeley, Ph.D.,
University of Minnesota Extension
Meteorologist and Climatologist,
Department of Soil, Water, and Climate,
St Paul, Minn.

BELLWETHER MEDIA · MINNEAPOLIS, MN

Marion Public Library
1095 6th Avenue
Marion, IA 52302-3428
(319) 377-3412

Note to Librarians, Teachers, and Parents:

Blastoff! Readers are carefully developed by literacy experts and combine standards-based content with developmentally appropriate text.

Level 1 provides the most support through repetition of high-frequency words, light text, predictable sentence patterns, and strong visual support.

Level 2 offers early readers a bit more challenge through varied simple sentences, increased text load, and less repetition of high-frequency words.

Level 3 advances early-fluent readers toward fluency through increased text and concept load, less reliance on visuals, longer sentences, and more literary language.

Level 4 builds reading stamina by providing more text per page, increased use of punctuation, greater variation in sentence patterns, and increasingly challenging vocabulary.

Level 5 encourages children to move from "learning to read" to "reading to learn" by providing even more text, varied writing styles, and less familiar topics.

Whichever book is right for your reader, Blastoff! Readers are the perfect books to build confidence and encourage a love of reading that will last a lifetime!

This edition first published in 2009 by Bellwether Media.

No part of this publication may be reproduced in whole or in part without written permission of the publisher. For information regarding permission, write to Bellwether Media Inc., Attention: Permissions Department, Post Office Box 19349, Minneapolis, MN 55419.

Library of Congress Cataloging-in-Publication Data
Manolis, Kay.
  Hurricanes / by Kay Manolis.
      p. cm. – (Blastoff! readers: Extreme weather)
  Includes bibliographical references and index.
  Summary: "Simple text and full color photographs introduce beginning readers to the characteristics of hurricanes. Developed by literacy experts for students in kindergarten through third grade"–Provided by publisher.
    ISBN-13: 978-1-60014-185-0 (hardcover : alk. paper)
    ISBN-10: 1-60014-185-4 (hardcover : alk. paper)
  1. Hurricanes–Juvenile literature. I. Title.

  QC944.2.M36 2008
  551.55'2–dc22   2008015218

Text copyright © 2009 by Bellwether Media Inc. BLASTOFF! READERS and associated logos are trademarks and/or registered trademarks of Bellwether Media Inc.

SCHOLASTIC, CHILDREN'S PRESS, and associated logos are trademarks and/or registered trademarks of Scholastic Inc. Printed in the United States of America.

Contents

What Is a Hurricane?

It is a beautiful summer day in the **tropics**.
The bright sun warms the ocean water.
This peaceful setting is perfect for
the start of a hurricane.

Hurricanes are huge, spinning storms that begin over warm ocean water near the **equator**.

Marion Public Library
1095 6th Avenue
Marion, IA 52302-3428
(319) 377-3412

How Do Hurricanes Form?

cool air moves in

warm air rises

warm ocean water

Hurricanes need **moisture** to get started. They start over warm, deep water. The air above this water is warm and full of moisture.

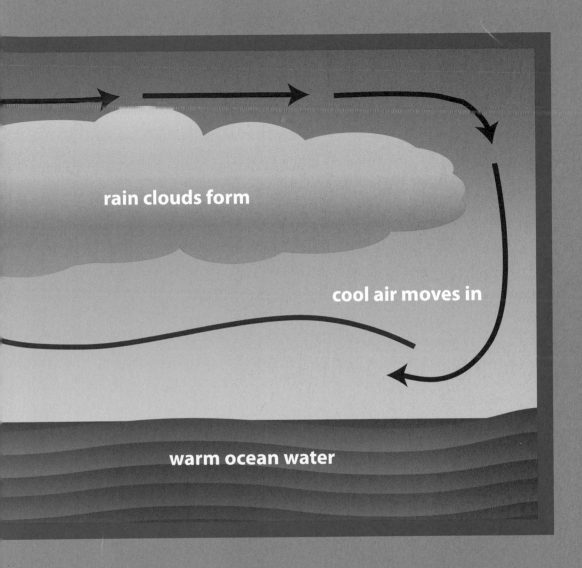

rain clouds form

cool air moves in

warm ocean water

Warm air is also light. It rises in the sky. Warm air cools as it rises. Cool air cannot hold as much moisture as warm air. When warm air rises, its moisture turns into rain clouds.

Hurricanes bring wind. When warm air rises, cool air rushes in to take its place. This air movement is wind.

fast fact

Hurricanes and tropical storms are the only storms that get their own names. Each one is given a name from an alphabetical list. Names can be used more than once, but the names for extremely bad hurricanes that strike land are never used again.

Wind and rain clouds can form a **tropical storm**. This is a storm with strong winds, but not as strong as hurricane winds. Hurricanes start as tropical storms.

A hurricane is a tropical storm that has gained strength. Hurricane winds move faster than 74 miles (119 kilometers) per hour.

fast fact

The winds in a tropical storm move between 39 and 73 miles (62 and 118 kilometers) per hour.

Scientists rank hurricanes by wind speed. There are five categories. A category 5 hurricane is the strongest. Its winds move more than 155 miles (249 kilometers) per hour.

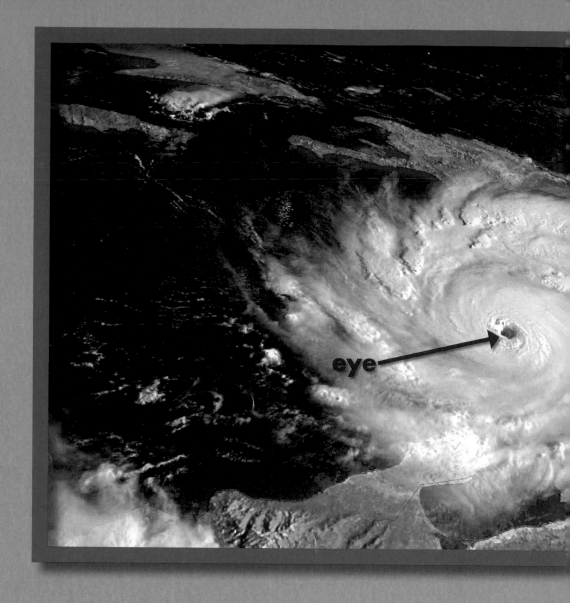

eye

Hurricane winds move in a spiral. They rotate around a central point where the **air pressure** is very low. This is the **eye** of the hurricane.

! **fast fact**
Hurricanes spin clockwise in the southern hemisphere and counterclockwise in the northern hemisphere. They never cross the equator.

The weather may be calm and the sky may be clear inside the eye. The most dangerous part of the hurricane is next to the eye. This is the **eye wall**. The storm's strongest winds are in this area.

What Can Hurricanes Do?

Hurricanes can travel a long distance over the ocean. They die out if they move over cool water. Most hurricanes end this way. Some keep moving over warm water.

The water's warmth and moisture fuel the hurricane's winds and rain clouds. These hurricanes keep moving and may hit land.

Hurricanes can cause serious damage on
land. The place where they first touch land
is usually most damaged. Hurricanes can
knock down trees and destroy buildings.

They also bring a **storm surge**. This is a sudden rise in the ocean's water level. The storm surge hits land like a huge, powerful wave. It can cause terrible floods.

Measuring and Predicting Hurricanes

Meteorologists try to predict a hurricane's path. They use satellites and **radar** to help them. They try to predict where the storm will hit land. Then people in its path can take steps to stay safe.

People may cover windows to keep them from being broken by wind or flying objects. The government may also order an **evacuation**. This tells people to move out of an area that is probably in the storm's path.

Marion Public Library
1095 6th Avenue
Marion, IA 52302-3428
(319) 377-3412

Hurricane Katrina

Hurricane Katrina was a very powerful storm that hit the southern coast of the United States in 2005. It destroyed buildings, roads, and homes. It also caused terrible floods. Many people lost their lives to this fierce hurricane.

Thankfully, hurricanes cannot continue for long once they move over a big body of land. The land cannot provide the warmth and moisture that the ocean provided to fuel the storms. They soon die out. Then clean-up begins. Hurricanes can leave behind incredible destruction.

Glossary

air pressure—the force of the air pressing down on Earth

equator—the imaginary line that circles the middle of the earth and divides the earth into two equal parts

evacuation—the act of leaving an area in order to stay safe

eye—the calm center point of a hurricane; the winds and rain clouds of a hurricane always move in a spiral around the eye.

eye wall—the edge of a hurricane's eye; the eye wall contains a hurricane's strongest winds.

meteorologists—scientists who forecast weather

moisture—water in the form of a gas that floats freely in the air

radar—a tool that uses radio waves to track weather conditions

storm surge—a sudden rise in ocean water during a hurricane; the rise is caused by the wind pushing the water into huge waves and piling it up onshore.

tropical storm—a spinning storm that forms over warm oceans near the equator; tropical storms have wind speeds of 39 to 74 miles (62 to 118 kilometers) per hour.

tropics—the hot and wet area of the earth that runs along both the north and south sides of the equator

To Learn More

AT THE LIBRARY

Berger Melvin and Gilda. *Hurricanes Have Eyes But Can't See and Other Amazing Facts about Wild Weather.* New York: Scholastic, 2003.

Hopping, Lorraine Jean. *Hurricanes!* New York: Scholastic, 1995.

Simon, Seymour. *Hurricanes.* New York: HarperCollins, 2003.

ON THE WEB

Learning more about hurricanes is as easy as 1, 2, 3.

1. Go to www.factsurfer.com

2. Enter "hurricanes" into search box.

3. Click the "Surf" button and you will see a list of related web sites.

With factsurfer.com, finding more information is just a click away.

Index

The images in this book are reproduced through the courtesy of: Meghan Pusey Diaz, front cover, pp. 14-15; Gregor Kervina, pp. 4-5; Linda Clavel, pp. 6-7; Jeff Greenberg / age fotostock, pp. 8-9, 16, 18, 21 (inset); AFP / Getty Images, pp. 10-11; Michael Braun, p. 11 (inset); Juan Martinez, pp. 12-13; David Olsen / Alamy, p. 17; Jim Reed / Getty Images, p. 19; Joseph Nickischer, pp. 20-21.